SOUTH CAROLINA'S
LOWCOUNTRY

Unforgettable Vintage Images of the Palmetto State

Note from the Publisher

Royalties from the sale of this book and the others in the Best of Series will be donated to the National Trust for Historic Preservation. These funds will be used to further their work and provide support to the preservation movement nationwide.

SOUTH CAROLINA'S
LOWCOUNTRY

Unforgettable Vintage Images of the Palmetto State

ARCADIA
PUBLISHING

Copyright © 2000 by Arcadia Publishing
ISBN 978-1-5316-6565-4

Published by Arcadia Publishing
Charleston, South Carolina

Library of Congress Catalog Card Number: 00-104648

For all general information contact Arcadia Publishing at:
Telephone 843-853-2070
Fax 843-853-0044
E-mail sales@arcadiapublishing.com
For customer service and orders:
Toll-Free 1-888-313-2665

Visit us on the Internet at www.arcadiapublishing.com

CONTENTS

ACKNOWLEDGMENTS

Arcadia would like to thank the following individuals for their contributions

Authors

Julia Cart	*Edisto Island: And I'm Glad*
Sherry Cawley	*Around Walterboro*
Anthony Chibbaro	*South Carolina's Lowcountry*
Coastal Discovery Museum	*Hilton Head Island*
Nathan Cole	*The Road to Hunting Island*
Edisto Island Historical Preservation Society	*Edisto Island*
Mary Moore Jacoby	*Charleston*
Thomas L. Johnson	*South Carolina Postcards Volume I, II, and III*
Ramona LaRoche	*Georgetown County*
Nick Lindsay	*Edisto Island: And I'm Glad*
John W. Meffert	*Charleston*
Mary Julia C. Royall	*Mount Pleasant*
Howard Woody	*South Carolina Postcards Volume I, II, and III*

Arcadia would like to thank the following groups for their contributions

Organizations, Historical Societies, and Businesses

Adventure Inn
Alcoa South Carolina Inc
Archivio Ugo Mulas
Barnwell Museum
Beaufort County Library
Beaufort Museum
Brookgreen Gardens Archives
Charleston City Hall
Charleston County Public Library
Charleston Museum
Colleton County Chamber of Commerce
Colleton County Historical & Preservation Society
Crowne Plaza
Disney's Hilton Head Island Resort
Duke University Special Collections Library
Exposure 60
First Presbyterian Church
Gay Seafood Company
Georgetown County Library
Georgia Historical Society
Hampton County Historical Museum
Hargray Communications

Hilton Head Historical Society
Hilton Head Island Medical Center
Hilton Head Island Middle School
Island Rentals and Real Estate
Jasper County Historical Society
The Library of Congress
Marriot Grand Ocean
Museum on the Common
Palmetto Electric Cooperative
Parris Island Museum
Press and Standard Newspaper
Pro Photo
Self Family Arts Center
Shem Creek Maritime Museum
South Carolinian Library
South Carolina Chamber of Commerce
South Carolina African American Heritage Council
South Carolina Department of Archives and History
Technical College of the Lowcountry
U.S. Army Military History Institute
University of South Carolina
Western Reserve Historical Society
Westin Resort

INTRODUCTION

Few places in the world harbor as much beauty, romanticism, culture, and history as does South Carolina's Lowcountry. A canvas of sorts for an incredible living painting, the Lowcountry is a rich and eclectic mixture of many schools of artistic expression. The region's lush marshlands provide a distinctly impressionist experience, with soft brushstrokes illustrating the meandering tidal creeks and swaying sea grass in a thousand shades of blue and green. A more classical and post-modern eye would see the stark lines and ornate designs in the Lowcountry dwellings and buildings, a rich gallery of different architectural tastes, from the pragmatic to the ornate. Together, the natural splendor and urban silhouette create a landscape unique in this nation's memory.

However, it is a region's people that sculpt the countryside, supplying the personality to the homes and to the structures, and the very charm to the villages and cities. The Lowcountry is blessed with many faces, both humble and noble, and it is the diverse nature of these men and women—patriot, Loyalist, rebel, unionist, slave, aristocrat, merchant, clergy—that have shaped the region's history over the past 300 years, from its earliest days as an experimental colony under the eight Lords Proprietors through the incendiary days of the Civil War to the present, a time of economic evolution and growth.

This pictorial compilation, a collection of the finest historical images from several previously published volumes by Arcadia Publishing, celebrates the traditions and history of the Lowcountry. These photographs and postcards allow today's readers a rare opportunity to step back into the past and view life as it was on the plantation, on the local farm, within a variety of small towns, and within the city, such as Charleston and Beaufort. From the Gullah communities on the region's picturesque Sea Islands to the stunning Battery Row homes in downtown Charleston, this book provides access to both the black and white societies, two worlds that were paradoxically separate, yet at all times intertwined. Through these photographs, the true character of the Lowcountry unfolds—an identity as complex as the intricate design of a sweetgrass basket. And it is in these same images that one can understand the strength of its people's character: the resilience and confidence to rebuild and continue after the devastation of war and natural disasters, such as earthquakes and seasonal hurricanes.

Over the past several years, Arcadia Publishing has produced nearly a dozen titles featuring the Lowcountry and its many different communities, from Edisto Island to the more commercially developed Hilton Head Island, from the smaller towns of Mount Pleasant and Walterboro to the larger cities of Beaufort and Charleston. Each previous book has captured, in word and image, only a part of the Lowcountry experience, and it is Arcadia's hope that this collection will provide readers up and down the Carolina coastline and beyond an opportunity to view the region not as an outsider, but as a local, full of the area's history and lore, and most importantly, the Lowcountry's magic.

Mark Berry
Editor, Arcadia Publishing

One

THE MILITARY

Members of the 3rd New Hampshire Regiment Band were a few of the nearly 30,000 Union troops living on Hilton Head Island from 1861 to 1865. These men decorated their living area with a few items picked up along the beach. Whelk shells and palmetto fronds are scattered in front of the tent. (Coastal Discovery Museum-Library of Congress.)

Shown here are Confederate ordinance officers in the process of inspecting the damage done to Fort Sumter by the Floating Battery, a floating gun platform placed in Charleston Harbor by Confederate forces. Officials of the young Confederacy were quick to survey their newly occupied position in order to make it defensible. The Union forces inside Sumter had been exposed to a bombardment that lasted 34 hours and consisted of over 3,000 rounds. Amazingly, there were no Union fatalities. However, two Yankee soldiers were killed during the flag-lowering ceremonies after the surrender. A 100-gun salute had been negotiated by Union commander Anderson, during which there was a mishap that caused a pile of powder cartridges to explode. The explosion killed one gunner on the spot and wounded a second, who died the following day. The dismounted gun in the foreground may have been caused by excessive recoil upon firing or by damage from incoming shells.

Posing by their cannons, Confederate soldiers, assumed by some to be members of the Palmetto Light Infantry, demonstrate their readiness and resolve to defend the fledgling Confederacy. Other researchers, however, have identified the unit as Company I of the Charleston Light Infantry. Regardless of the identity of the militia unit depicted in the photograph, it is a fact that hundreds of Charleston families contributed sons to such units, which, in turn, saw action in many battles in the Charleston area during the war. The topography of the land in the photograph suggests that it may have been taken near Fort Pemberton, on the western side of James Island. If so, that would be the Stono River in the background. But some researchers hold that the setting could be the Confederate fortifications on Cole's Island, before the works were abandoned in 1862. (George S. Cook, photographer; courtesy of John Steele.)

This widely reproduced view of the Fort Sumter Parade Grounds in April 1861 shows Confederate dignitaries inspecting a Columbiad cannon that was poised to fire on downtown Charleston. Major Robert Anderson, commander of the beleaguered Union forces inside Sumter, had ordered that this cannon, along with several others, be positioned like a mortar and be made ready to fire on the city itself. Fortunately, he never gave the final order to fire. The tall gentleman in the top hat, standing closest to the cannon, has long been thought to be Wade Hampton, a man who was to become a successful Confederate general and, later, a popular governor of South Carolina. However, he is not mentioned as having visited the fort in any of the many newspaper reports of the day. Contemporary media accounts do place then-governor Francis Pickens at the fort on April 14, along with Colonel F.J. Moses Jr., J.L. Dearing, Chancellor Carroll, and Judges Glover and Wardlaw. Note the hot shot furnace standing immediately behind the group.

This photograph, taken c. 1865, shows the deck and turret of the Monitor *Catskill*. Fort Sumter received heavy fire not only from the Union fortifications on Morris Island, but also from the blockading fleet. Beginning in the spring of 1863, the Union fleet could call upon the services of several of its new class of ironclad warships. Based out of Port Royal during the war were the monitors *Weehawken*, *Passaic*, *Keokuk*, *Nahant*, *Nantucket*, *Patapsco*, *Montauk*, and *Catskill*. Sporting two large guns inside their heavily armored turrets, each ship could fire at Sumter and Moultrie and feel almost impregnable to return fire. But despite its seeming edge, the Union fleet was never able to blast its way past the main harbor defenses. In this view, the staff of the *Catskill* poses for the photographer. The commanding officer of the ship, Lieutenant Commander Edward Barrett, is seated atop the turret, while the remainder of his staff strike poses elsewhere on the deck. Note the two small cannon at each side of the turret and the four shells that appear in the foreground.

"Every morning in Beaufort town," the editor of the *Beaufort Gazette* observed on September 7, 1917, "the rifle practice of the Marines on Paris Island can be heard and the Boches [Germans] will soon have cause to know that this training in marksmanship is not to be scorned." Part of every Marine recruit's basic training was weapons instruction on the rifle range and in the trenches. An expert rifleman could increase his monthly pay by $5.

According to Major McClellan, Marines and Naval personnel have together been connected with the history of Paris Island since 1861, when as joint Federal forces under command of Flag Officer Samuel Francis DuPont, they took possession of the forts and surrounding territory on Bay Point and Hilton Head. This postcard demonstrates better than most the subsequent mutual dependency of these two branches of the armed services in the area, both often relying upon the presence of the other to do their jobs—and for their jobs.

An essential part of "Mainside" Paris Island, the dock, or boat landing, on the Beaufort River was the main entry point for personnel and supplies until 1928, when the bridge was built across Archer's Creek, thus connecting the causeway and Horse Island. The large open-sided shed still stands on the dock as a remnant of the structures that were part of the waterside apparatus of an earlier day.

The castellated neo-Gothic Beaufort Arsenal is believed to have been constructed in 1795 on the site of the town's first courthouse. It was rebuilt in 1852 after severe fire damage to its upper story. For many years the Arsenal was home to the Beaufort Volunteer Artillery, the fifth oldest military unit in the United States. Remodeled and furnished by the Women's Civic League during World War I, it became known as the Beaufort Sojourners' Club and served as a recreation center for enlisted men from Paris Island. Today the Arsenal, as the Beaufort Museum, houses a small but valuable collection of historical artifacts and relics of local and regional importance.

Marion Whaley served in the Army Air Corps during the Second World War. When he retired, he returned to Edisto and opened South Point Services, a convenience store on Edisto Beach. Whaley served as mayor of Edisto Beach and was a familiar figure to vacationers who spent their summers and holidays there.

Captain Joseph Elias King (1917–1952) is pictured here during World War II. After the war, he returned to Georgetown County and taught algebra at Howard High School.

These four Marines stand in front of one of the only stores on Hilton Head Island in the 1940s. Mose Hudson ran this store located near the Jenkins Island ferry dock. The Hudson store was not just a place to purchase necessities, it also became a popular spot for socializing. (Courtesy Barbara Hudson.)

World War II flying ace, Beverly "Bevo" Howard performs his daredevil airplane show off the Battery in this undated photo. Here, "Bevo" flies upside down to pick up a ribbon held by the man standing on the dock. (The Charleston Museum Collection, MK 20315.)

When they were not learning how to use this 3-inch anti-aircraft gun, this group of Marines found out that it made a good perch. (Courtesy Barbara Hudson.)

Confederate Monument,
Walterboro, S. C.

On June 22, 1911, the Confederate Veterans of Colleton County dedicated the Confederate Monument on the Courthouse Square. The 32-foot structure cost $1,000 and over 50 Confederate veterans were in attendance. The first inscription says, "To the Confederate Soldiers of Colleton County; To those who fought and lived; Those who fought and died; To those who gave much and to those who gave all." The second inscription states, "To the mothers, wives, sisters and daughters of Colleton County who fought the home battles of 1861–1865." The monument has been in three locations around the Courthouse. As the postcards indicate, it has been at the corner of Jefferies Boulevard and Hampton Street, on the corner of East Washington and Waters Street across from the old Vogler Hotel, and in the center of the Courthouse facing Hampton Street.

"The Fallen of the Mighty Conflict—Graves of Confederate Soldiers, Charleston, S.C.," reads the caption printed on this turn-of-the-century view. These ladies were not yet born when Charleston's youngest and brightest were asked to serve their country. Scores of Charlestonians died gallantly in the war, including many of the 800 that were buried here in South Carolina's only official Confederate cemetery. Most of those interred at Magnolia were killed in defense of the city of Charleston, but 84 were South Carolinians who lost their lives at the battle of Gettysburg. Five Confederate brigadier generals were also buried at Magnolia, along with the second crew of the C.S.S. *Hunley*, which included Horace L. Hunley, the submarine's designer. (Underwood & Underwood.)

Two

OUT TO SEA

Picnic and parking areas were located just off the Hunting Island beach inside the forest. Visitors could, until the 1970s, park next to an empty table, thus claiming it for the day. One bit of sport among frequent "day trippers" was to watch a first-time visitor become stuck in a sand bed and then assist the driver in freeing the trapped vehicle.

The Ocean Villa, a friendly beach boardinghouse owned by Harvie and Jennie Lybrand, was an important social center on Edisto Beach. People came in the summer from far and near for their little glimpse of "heaven on earth," staying in the villa and enjoying hours of lazing away the warm summer days interrupted only by delicious meals. Many former guests acquired beach houses and continue to come to Edisto, bringing their "grans" and "great grans."

A row boat like this, with a pointed bow, square stern, and flat bottom, was sometimes referred to as a bateau. The tide comes in rapidly, so the ladies would not have to wait long before they are afloat. Sullivan's Island is in the background to the right.

In this image, one can see the high dunes that were once a familiar sight on Edingsville and the horses, carriage, and passengers pausing during their "process" down the beach. In 1874, Edingsville was visited by a hurricane which swept away all of the buildings but three. An earthquake in 1886 and another hurricane in 1893 moved Edingsville into the ocean, and its bones now lie a half mile out to sea.

In 1903, a boat with several passengers sets out from Cantini's Warf at the foot of Rutledge Avenue at Tradd Street, before the construction of Murray Boulevard. (The Charleston Museum Collection, MK 17541.)

The arrival of wealthy Northerners who owned hunting estates and partnership shooting clubs in the Lowcountry helped put Charleston on the map. Airplane service to and from the city was just beginning when this 1935 view was taken, and there were discussions of having regular hydroplane service to Charleston. A Pan American flight hydroplane is docked in the harbor, below the recently opened Cooper River Bridge. (The Charleston Museum Collection, MK 915.)

Riding on the beach was not prohibited in the 1930s. The pharmacist and his friends are ready to launch the boat for a day's fishing. His daughter, sitting on the boat, was the "birthday girl."

Boating was a social event for which the ladies dressed in their best attire. Styles were quite feminine with lovely long skirts. Bouffant hairdos were covered with wide-brimmed hats to protect the fair complexions.

Bathing suits have certainly changed in design from the styles worn by these prospective swimmers. Sunscreen had not been developed. Broad-brimmed hats protected complexions instead.

The pavilion at the Isle of Palms was the highlight of a day trip to the beach. Four young women in bathing costumes make a dash for the water in a photograph made in the early part of the century. (The Charleston Museum Collection, MK 14684A.)

Style on the Isle of Palms in 1902 is evidenced by a display of beachwear: (from left to right) Katie Waring, Tom Buist, Rena Smith, I.G. Ball, J.H. Ball [?], unidentified, Miriam Todd, Billy Smith, Helen McIver, Glover Alston, and unidentified. (The Charleston Museum Collection, MK 9988.)

Elizabeth McPherson Gregorie Sams, Francis Gregorie Sams, Lili Gregorie, and Donald Dean Sams enjoy the beach in this view taken by Dr. Franklin Frost Sams in July 1903. (The Charleston Museum Collection, MK 7776.)

Water excursions from Charleston were a very popular diversion. In this photograph, taken in 1919, the *Vadie*, owned by H.P. Williams, is moored near Pompion Hill Chapel on the Cooper River. (The Charleston Museum Collection, MK 4324.)

The small village of Rockville at the end of Wadmalaw Island hosts the Rockville Regatta in August, one of the long-standing Lowcountry traditions. In this 1936 view, the race committee observes competitors as they made the turn in front of the Yacht Club. (The Charleston Museum Collection, MK 7349H.)

This pre-1907 card shows, at left, the two-story clapboard house which burned in 1907 and was replaced in 1909 by the concrete stone block Victorian residence at 607 Bay erected by William Joseph Thomas. The Waterhouse home, at right, built by Lewis Reeve Sams in 1852, was reportedly saved from the fire by the bucket-brigade efforts of the Waterhouse cotton gin workers, who also used wet blankets to beat out the flames.

Here, in this 1893 view of White Point Gardens, a civilized gentleman enjoys the quiet of the waterfront. The city was active in parks improvement. Planting became a major civic activity, balancing the trees that were being cut down to allow for electric lines and telephone poles. Note the city bathhouse in the distance. (The Charleston Museum Collection, MK 22902, AWC.)

As Reconstruction was visited upon the former Confederacy, the city of Charleston seemed to have a tougher time than most of the other war-ravaged Southern cities. Situated on a peninsula overlooking a large harbor at the mouths of two rivers, the city attempted to use its geographical advantages to recapture its former status as the premier commercial port of the Southeast. Even with thousands of bales of cotton and thousands of sacks of rice beginning to move again through the port city on their way to distant destinations, it would be many years before Charleston would be even a semblance of her former self. This view shows bales of cotton sitting on the Cooper River wharves, waiting to be loaded onto cargo ships. (Standard Series.)

After the rice was milled, it was placed in sacks to be shipped. Shown in this photo are dock hands transporting sacks of rice to the waiting ships. (Kilburn Brothers, publishers; courtesy of Len Ances.)

The two ocean-going, gas-powered St. Augustine trawlers shown here, center and right, with their nets suspended aft, are tied up on Coffin Creek, on the northeastern end of St. Helena Island near the shrimp-rich waters off Egg Bank. In 1928, Beaufort was the center of the state's fledgling shrimping industry with 96 licensed shrimp boats and nets (as opposed to 13 for Charleston and 3 for Georgetown), an increase of 46 over 1927. The craft at left appears to be a convered yacht.

F.W. arrives at the dock from Sullivan's Island. This 1905 photograph documents the *Sappho*, a ferry that ran between Charleston and Sullivan's Island before the Cooper River Bridge was built. The Cadillac, said to be that which transported President Taft on his visit to the exposition in 1901/02, sits next to the more mundane, but equally important, bags of rice. (The Charleston Museum Collection, MK 14788.)

One of the most popular Lowcountry pastimes is the oyster roast. Such a roast can feed hundreds or just a few like this one after a hunting expedition in the early 1950s. (Coastal Discovery Museum.)

For decades, oystermen have depended upon harvesting oysters from area waterways for survival during the oyster season (from September to April). Picking oysters was (and is) almost always done by men. Oystermen land their boats on the oyster rakes and gather the oysters using tongs as well as their hands. The work is muddy and can be dangerous. Oyster shells are very sharp and can easily cut unprotected hands. (*Island Packet.*)

Once the oysters were loaded into the bateaux, they were taken to the oyster factories and piled onto large tables. From the 1920s until the 1970s, several island families operated oyster factories. In the Hudson factory, over 250 gallons of oysters were shucked each day by the women working there. Workers were paid with Hudson money, which could only be used at the Hudson store. (Barbara Hudson.)

This group of fishermen displays one of the largest sand sharks found off Charleston waters in this 1929 photograph. The shark was caught off Porcher's Bluff, north of Mount Pleasant. (The Charleston Museum Collection, MK 20198.)

Fun is what one makes for oneself, as these boys demonstrate by aqua-planing on the harbor. "Happy" Paul and his dog test the waters while Robin Matthew (left), Billy Minott (center), and an unidentified boy enjoy the ride in September 1954. (The Charleston Museum Collection, MK 4863.)

Three

THE LOWCOUNTRY

Sweet potatoes were an important part of the plantation workers' diet. Here, freedmen are using hoes to pull them out of the ground at the Hopkinson's Cassina Point Plantation. The men are dressed in Federal uniforms, which were no doubt shared with them by the occupying soldiers. Note: This photograph, taken by the resident Federal army photographer, has been published many times with the location incorrectly identified.

The palmetto tree has long been another widely recognizable image representative of the South Carolina Lowcountry. From the time of the Revolutionary War, when palmetto logs were used to construct Fort Moultrie, to the present day, when the palmetto graces our state flag and lines the streets of Charleston, one cannot help but think of South Carolina when one sees a palmetto tree. Photographer J.A. Palmer of Aiken captured this lone palmetto overlooking a marsh at an unknown location. (J.A. Palmer.)

The cabbage palmetto is South Carolina's state tree. Its importance to the state is demonstrated by its placement on the state flag and seal. The tree was used by Colonial troops during the American Revolution on Sullivan's Island to build fortifications. The soft, springy wood repelled the shells from the British fleet and helped bring about a Colonial victory.

A family, dressed in their Sunday finery, rests under a palmetto tree. The serenity and slow-moving pace of this photo reminds the modern viewer that the days were not as hurried 130 years ago. (J.N. Wilson.)

This photograph above presents an extensive view of the graveyard of the "Brick Church." During Reconstruction the church became the focal point of educational, political, and religious activities for African Americans. And more recently, Martin Luther King Jr.'s "March on Washington" was planned right across the street at the Penn School. (Sam Cooley, photographer; courtesy of Marvin Housworth.)

Spanish moss is a non-parasitic plant that grows on the branches of trees. It gathers nourishment and water from atmospheric humidity and air borne dust. The Low Country trees abound with the plants which hang like pendants from the trees. In areas where the trees have overgrown the roadways, they form eerie, web-like tunnels.

The Ashepoo [ASH-e-POO as in boot] River starts below Walterboro and flows between the communities of Green Pond and Ashepoo above Highway 17 and finally runs into St. Helena Sound. Nearby plantations include Bonnie Doone, Poco Sabo, Lavington, and Airy Hall. Numerous fish are caught in the freshwater part of the river and many alligators make it their home. Today the Ashepoo is the "A" part of the ACE Basin.

The Edisto [ED-is-TOE] River is the longest free-flowing, black water river in North America. In the fresh water part of the river, one can fish for redbreast, brim, crappie, largemouth bass, and catfish. Rock fish and shad make runs into the freshwater to spawn. Shad roe is a Lowcountry delicacy. Below Willtown Bluff, the river becomes salt water and one can catch shrimp, crabs, oysters, flounder, and spot-tailed bass. Above Edisto Island, the river branches into the North and South forks, flowing on both sides of the Island into the Atlantic Ocean. Today the Edisto and the South fork of the Edisto River serve as one of Colleton County's boundary lines and is the "E" part of the ACE Basin. (Photo Arts, Winnsboro, South Carolina.)

Walking the log is what they were planning. Holding hands made it so much more secure as they precariously made their way.

Success! They made it all the way to the end of the fallen tree. Seated, they contemplate the rushing mountain stream beneath them. A question—where was the photographer?

These couples appear to be planning something. It is not clear what the significance of the empty water bucket is. They are at Melrose, near Hendersonville and Brevard, NC, a favorite vacation spot for people from Mount Pleasant.

A day in the country provided fun for the two couples and their dog. They appear to be hiding behind a hedgerow while their picture is taken by the other young gentleman.

Barbed wire presents no obstacle when two friends are nearby to hold the strands apart for the young lady. The photographer is the other girl. One might guess it is a Sunday afternoon since the boys are dressed in suits and hats. But note the straw the one on the left has in his mouth.

Two gentlemen partake of one of life's extras with bread and wine on a riverside picnic in this early 1900s photograph by M.B. Paine. (The Charleston Museum Collection, MK 14252.)

How wonderful for children when the weather turned warm and they could take off their heavy winter stockings and go down to the water's edge and go wading. "Miss Dolly's" house is to the right. Inside the harbor the water was calm and there were no dangerous holes. It was safe for youngsters.

This photograph was taken near Otranto Plantation on the Cooper River during the second auto outing of the Charleston Auto Club in 1910. An unidentified group of ladies realize the full benefit of their newfound independence, afforded by the horseless carriage. (The Charleston Museum Collection, MK 13525B.)

Tomotley Plantation Drive, between Beaufort and Walterboro, S. C.

This card states the location of Tomotley plantation is between Beaufort and Walterboro. While Tomotley I is in Beaufort County, most of the original barony granted to Landgrave Edmund Bellinger in the 1600s was in Colleton County. His other plantations included Tomotley II, Poco Sabo, Whitehouse, Rotherwood, and Bonnie Doone. Tomotley I was purchased by the Izard family in 1755. In 1820, Patience Izard is credited with planting the avenue of live oaks. Patience married Col. Abraham Eustis. James H. Bagget bought Tomotley in 1864. Although it was burned in 1865, there was an intriguing court battle after the Civil War between Bagget and the Eustis heirs that ended up in federal court. The plantation was sold a number of times and is owned today by Mr. and Mrs. William Mixon.

VE OAK AVENUE ON OLD DEHON RICE PLANTATION, WALTERBORO, S. C. D-599

About 1859, Dr. Theodore DeHon bought part of the Pringle property and named his plantation "DeHon." After the Civil War, it was owned by Cotesworth Pinckney Fishburne, who sold it it E. Louisa Fishburne in 1910. When A.S. Caspary bought over 15,000 acres in Colleton County in 1931, it included eight plantations and a number of land tracts. Two of these plantations were DeHon and Bonnie Doone. Mr. Caspary built his mansion of over 30 rooms where the DeHon plantation home had been before it was burned in 1865 by Sherman's troops. He renamed all his property Bonnie Doone.

Pon Pon Plantation dates back to the late 1600s. The plantation's lineage began with Sacheverell, then Skirving to Smith to Elliott. William and Ann Smith Elliott changed the name to Oak Lawn. Both were well educated, and together they ran a number of inherited plantations and raised nine children. Oak Lawn became their winter home. When his lands were confiscated during the Civil War, William burned all his crops rather than let them be used by the Union soldiers. He died in Charleston before the plantation was burned in 1865 by Sherman's troops. After the war, Ann and her daughters returned to Oak Lawn and lived in an old washroom/kitchen, as it was the only building left standing on the plantation. They lived there for many years as they began to revive what they could from their lands. At this time the land was still part of Colleton County.

The Civil War and its aftermath brought myriad changes to plantation life throughout the South, and the once-great rice plantations of the Lowcountry were no exceptions. Gone were the days of unhurried grandeur and unworried splendor, only to be replaced with a daily grind of sweat and hard work. Never again would wealthy landowners order their slaves out into the rice fields. Some of the former slaveowners lucky enough to still have their plantations now found themselves doing much of the planting and harvesting. And, unbeknownst to all, it would not be long before foreign competition and a couple of strong hurricanes would force the working rice plantation into the history books. In this view, two young African-American girls, possibly the children of former slaves, peer through the wrought iron gate of the Oaks Plantation. (Underwood & Underwood.)

It was from these sea island homes that the planters would mount week-long expeditions, at times accompanied by their family and slaves, to Hunting Island. The taking of deer, ducks, and other small game was not only a sport for the planter but served a practical purpose. While vegetables could be grown in gardens for food, these hunting trips were a major source of meat for the families on the plantations. A group of planters eventually purchased the southern end of Hunting Island for use as a private preserve.

The Cultbert House on Bay Street is an example of the many magnificent summer homes built in Beaufort by the planters. Edgar Fripp, a member of the largest family on the sea islands, built "Tidalholm," Paul Hamilton named his residence "The Oaks," and Robert Barnwell created his "Castle." Collectively, these houses, along with the great wealth they represented, made South Carolina's second oldest town the "most aristocratic" city in the South until the War Between the States. (Beaufort County Library.)

The "Golden Age" of the planters ended with the War Between the States, yet most of the plantations remained intact and undamaged due to the early Union occupation. This photograph of the Robert Fuller plantation, made in the spring of 1865, has a note on the back that reads, "Rob. Fuller plantation dwelling house on St. Helena Island. 5 miles from Beaufort on Wallace Creek. Now owned by E.S. Philbrick, Esq. & managed by T.E. Ruggles. T.E.R. & his sister are seen in this picture. This is a very pretty & cozy place. It is where I stayed in Sept. 1865 while keeping store for E.S.P." This is an unusual photograph, for very few historical documents about the planters remain. Union occupation troops seized the planter's personal and business records and shipped them north. Some planters transferred their memorabilia inland to Barnwell, Orangeburg, and Columbia, only to have them burned by Sherman's army. (Beaufort County Library.)

One Gullah tradition brought from Africa lived underground on the plantations. This was their religious belief in evil spirits and the magic of root medicine to cure or kill. This faith in the supernatural mixed with Christian dogma to form a hybrid religion. Root doctors were forbidden to practice their craft by the planters in fear that they would be poisoned. Yet, the practice has continued to the present, and Frogmore is considered to be one of the most powerful voodoo centers in America. The acceptance of spiritualism is so great that a past High Sheriff of Beaufort County was also a practicing root doctor because he often had to remove spells and curses before he could perform his legal duties. St. Helena is also where the famous root doctor, Dr. Buzzard, is buried. This belief in the supernatural is best exemplified by the story of the Graybeards.

The picture postcard was a perfect, inexpensive means of publicizing the architecture, way of life, achievements, and needs of an institution like Penn Normal, Industrial, and Agricultural School, located 8 miles from Beaufort on St. Helena Island. Founded in 1862 as a school for freed slaves, Penn became the center for promoting black islanders' education, welfare, health, and heritage. When P.W. Dawkins became the school's superintendent of industries early in the twentieth century, he made the 90-acre school farm a demonstration model and mandated the teaching of practical agriculture to all older pupils, most of whom were destined to become engaged in some phase of the small-farm economy which supported St. Helena.

Here is a generic greeting card showing black laborers harvesting turpentine. There actually was a turpentine industry in Colleton County from the 1920s to the 1940s. There were, at least, six turpentine distributors in the county, including two in Stokes and one each in Walterboro, Canadys, Smoaks, and Ruffin.

In 1949, a group of timber associates from Hinesville, Georgia, bought 20,000 acres of pine forest on Hilton Head's southern end. The Hilton Head Company was founded to manage the timber cutting. The four partners were Gen. Joseph B. Fraser, Fred C. Hack, (shown here), Olin T. McIntosh, and C.C. Stebbins. All of the men invested in the island for the timber. After the harvesting was complete, however, these visionaries turned their sights on developing the island. (The Fred C. Hack family.)

Once rice grains were separated from the plant, they would be placed into a mortar. The receptacle was made from a hollowed tree stump. The rice grains would then be pounded with a wooden pestle to remove the hull. During the period of slavery, it was not unusual for an enslaved person to be given the daily task of pounding seven mortar fills each day. Pictured are a woman and boy pounding rice during the early 1930s at Brookgreen. (Brookgreen Gardens Archives, Murrells Inlet, South Carolina.)

Abraham Herriot winnows rice as chickens feed. This picture was taken on Sandy Island in 1930. The winnowing of rice was initially done by hand using large woven sweet grass baskets, known as fanners. This was a tradition brought from West Africa. The rice was tossed in the air, allowing the wind to blow the chaff away. All parts of the rice plants were used; the stalks and stubble were used for animal bedding, and the chaff would be removed and used for animal feed. Although chaff left on the rice allows it to remain brown and produces the healthy substance of bran, it had to be removed to keep the rice from becoming rancid as bushels were exported around the world by ship. (Brookgreen Gardens Archives, Murrells Inlet, South Carolina.)

Edith Dabbs in *Face of an Island* (1970) identifies the woman in this picture as Mrs. Green, shown standing in front of her home adjoining Penn School property at the waterfront. The photograph was taken by Connecticut native Leigh Richmond Miner (1864–1935), whose work is the focus of Mrs. Dabbs's book.

When family groups began farming Hilton Head Island in the late 19th century, they had to grow enough food to support the entire family. There was little opportunity to purchase extra supplies. Tomatoes, potatoes, watermelon, sugar cane, squash, peas, butterbeans, citrus fruit, and numerous other crops were grown on the island for nearly a century. Most of the work had to be done by hand or with limited animal power even through the 1950s when this photo was taken. (Elizabeth Grant.)

Helen Bryan is one of the only remaining cast net makers on Hilton Head Island. In the past, it was very common for people to produce handmade nets. She hand ties each knot in the net, which is used for catching fish and shrimp. (*Island Packet*-Jay Karr.)

Spanish moss drapes the cypress trees in this Lowcountry forest in Dorchester County. Sometimes called "old man's beard," the hanging plant is really neither moss nor vine. Belonging to the same botanical family as the pineapple, the "moss" actually gains its sustenance from the air and not its host tree. (Keystone View Company.)

Baskets had always been essential to the residents of isolated St. Helena, where since plantation times the people had made and used them as their basic containers and carriers. The ancient art and science of making baskets was kept alive at Penn through the services of craftsmen who passed down their skills from generation to generation. Edith Dabbs mentions two such teachers at the school: Alfred Graham, who learned basket-making from his grand-uncle who had brought it from Africa, and his grand-nephew George Brown. Their baskets were considered excellent.

Sea oats are found in the more hostile environment of the primary dunes which are closest to salt water. Seeds from the plants are carried by the wind and deposited along the dune line to start new colonies. Because of the importance of the sea oats to the building and stabilization of sand dunes, the plant is under federal protection.

Sea oats are a special type of grass which help protect the sand dunes. It is one of the a very few plants which is salt tolerant and resistant to the severe beach conditions, thus making it able to survive along and on a dune line. Its tap roots penetrate several feet into the ground in search of water, and the leaves at the base form a bush-like structure which catches and holds sand.

The maritime forest is located in the interior of Hunting Island behind the dunes. It is one of the few undisturbed forests left in South Carolina. The forest contains a great diversity of bush plants and trees. These plants are not salt tolerant and must be protected from salt spray by the dunes. The trees, especially the hardwoods, provide life support for migrating birds in the spring and fall. Birds can find a wide variety of insects on which to feed, along with fruit from the wax myrtle, palmetto, magnolia, and holly. The maritime forest has been subject to damage from strong storms, fires, and erosion to the point where there are few large trees left on the island.

Much of the land in the maritime forest is low lying and swampy. When the spring rains arrive, stagnant water collects in these areas. These swamps become breeding grounds for mosquitoes. Though malaria, a mosquito-borne disease, is no longer a major problem, the pests can make human life very uncomfortable during the spring and summer.

Damage to the maritime forest didn't end when the storms were over. Tree root systems were weakened by the removal of the sand, allowing trees to be blown over more easily when the next storm hit. Also, the trees were not salt tolerant, and salt spray blown from the ocean on the tree roots greatly reduced the trees' chances for survival. (South Carolina Archives and History.)

At the end of the 1920s, a group of local citizens began a movement to make Hunting Island into a county park. Once the three different owners had donated the land to Beaufort County in the mid-1930s, the work began. A major part of the process of transforming the island was constructing a means of motorized access to the island. The St. Helena road ended at the edge of the marshes near the Harbor River. Causeways had to be built across the salt marshes, and bridges had to be erected over the Harbor River and Johnson's Creek. This costly project would have been impossible during the years of the Great Depression without the assistance of the Civilian Conservation Corps (CCC). This New Deal Program was started to help ease the country's financial difficulties, and in the process, the CCC built seventeen state parks in South Carolina alone.

The heart of Magnolia Cemetery was always a favorite destination for picnics and outings. Families vied with each other to produce monuments worthy of their lineage. Fine examples of stone sculpture and cast iron may be found on the grounds. Magnolia Cemetery continues to serve as a choice resting spot for many Charlestonians. (The Charleston Museum Collection, MK 22907, AWC.)

The old docks near the Batter provided an open space for children to fly kites. M.B. Paine captured these lads enjoying the breeze off the harbor in 1930. (The Charleston Museum Collection, MK 9094.)

Sand dunes are an important feature in the construction of a barrier island. Dune construction is greatest during the summer months when the winds and water are calmer. Sand is distributed across the beach by the wind until it is deposited against some obstacle. The dunes are fundamental to protecting the maritime forest and salt marsh from flooding by the surf and severe storms which blow in from the ocean. Due to a high erosion rate, there are few natural sand dunes remaining on Hunting Island except at the northern end of the island. Marine Corps bulldozers spent the beginning months of 1997 pushing up sand at South Beach to form new dunes in order to replace those lost to storms.

The primary dunes are almost totally gone at the center of Hunting Island, and there are very few secondary dunes remaining. The sea oats have migrated inland to what is left of the secondary dune line and maritime forest and are replacing the less salt-tolerant plants, such as wax myrtle and live oaks.

A very young Tom Peeples enjoys Hilton Head Island's water in 1955. He probably had no idea that the very island he visited would eventually be home to over 30,000 people and that he would be the town's mayor. (Mary Ann Peeples.)

71

From the 1890s through the 1950s, Hilton Head was visited in the winter season by hunting parties searching for game. The Clydes, Hurleys, Thornes, and Loomises used parts of the island as private retreats. Turkey, quail, doves, duck, and other wild fowl were prevalent. Deer, mink, wild boar, alligators, and occasionally, snakes were also the hunters' targets. Will Clyde stands with his guide, Tommy Wright, who shows off the rattlesnake that Clyde hunted. (Fred C. Hack family.)

In 1917, a group of North Carolina hunters began buying property near present-day Palmetto Dunes for a hunting lodge. They amassed 2,000 acres and called themselves the Hilton Head Agricultural Club because they intended to grow limited amounts of cotton. Their agricultural pursuits were unsuccessful. By the 1930s, there were over 40 members associated through business and family connections. Some Chattanoogans were also included, although the core group of members came from near Gastonia, North Carolina. This photograph was taken in front of the clubhouse during the 1939 hunt. Members met in Savannah for an annual banquet and then rode the *Clivedon*, the ferry, to Hilton Head the next morning. (Charles S. Thompson scrapbook.)

"Our hunting grounds can be rented for a very small amount, thousands of acres are rented by Northern sportsmen whom we always welcome into our sunny Southland," R.B. Vance would write about Allendale County in the late 1930s. "We never hear of one violating our game laws and this is why we are glad to see them; too, it helps the farmer to pay his taxes on his outlying land." This could have been said of the entire region during the two preceding decades as well.

On some occasions, Hilton Head Agricultural Club members brought their families along for the fun. These children posed next to one of the day's trophies; they are, from left to right, as follows: (front row) Mary K. Winget and Anna Boyce Rankin; (back row) Bob Van Sleen, Margaret McConnell, Tom Thompson, and Grady Rankin. (Charles S. Thompson scrapbook.)

Four

STRUCTURES

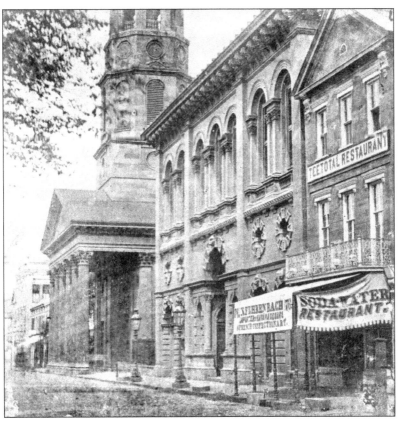

Above is Secession Hall and the Circular Congregational Church, Meeting Street, c. 1861. The building in the center of the view above was the home of the South Carolina Institute, an early mechanical and agricultural society headquartered in downtown Charleston. In December of 1860 and partly in response to Abraham Lincoln being elected president, the State of South Carolina voted to secede from the Union. The Ordinance of Secession, the document which put the Palmetto State on a collision course with the North and paved the way for the onset of the Civil War, was signed in the Institute's hall. The building then became popularly known as Secession Hall. This photo was probably taken in late 1860, just after the signing of the Ordinance, or in 1861, as all the buildings pictured were virtually destroyed in the Great Fire of the latter year. The Circular Church appears on the left. (Fred VonSanten.)

A.A Heyward built his home in the latest Victorian fashion. The house stood at 11 Legare Street in the heart of the old downtown district, at the corner of Gibbes and Legare Streets. Enjoying some success despite a general downturn in Charleston's economy, Mr. Heyward was listed in the 1893 city directory simply as a "Planter." The house survived through the 1940s as apartments, but was torn down in the 1950s. (The Charleston Museum Collection, MK 22695, AWC.)

M.B. Paine photographed this view from the piazza of the Edmonston-Alston House. This wonderful picture shows a cruise ship leaving the harbor, evocative of Charleston's connection to a larger world. (The Charleston Museum Collection, MK 9688.)

These two homes on South Battery have very historic pasts. The house on the left, at 20 South Battery, was built *c.* 1843 by Samuel N. Stevens and was remodeled after the war by Colonel Richard Lathers. Lathers, a native of Georgetown, had gone to New York as a young man and had become wealthy as a cotton broker and banker. During the Civil War, he served in the Union army. After the war he returned to the South and purchased this house. Inviting many military and political leaders to elegant receptions at his mansion, he hoped to bring about a quick reconciliation between Northerners and Southerners. A few years later, discouraged, he gave up the attempt and returned to the North. The home on the right, at 1 Meeting Street, was built *c.* 1846 and at one time housed the Ross Museum, containing the art collections of the Ross family. Note the trolley parked at the intersection in this interesting period view. (George N. Barnard, photographer; courtesy of Marvin Housworth.)

This daguerreotype of the Siegling Music House at 243 King Street was made in the mid-1800s. The posed nature of the scene was not an accident, as exposures could take minutes. This image represents one of the earliest photographs in The Charleston Museum Collection (MK 8986).

The McKinley house, dating from about 1878, no longer stands. It was located in Hilliardsville, where Pierates Cruze homes are. Looking toward the city, you can see the ferry wharfs. After the Dana Osgoods purchased it in 1928, they developed Pierates Cruze Gardens on the property. Azaleas and camellias added beauty, but most spectacular was the panoramic view of the harbor.

Owned by the Burckmyer family during this period, the residence at 501 Pinckney Street had been built c. 1810–1814 by Dr. James Robert Verdier, known for his successful treatment of yellow fever patients. During the Civil War it was used as the headquarters of the U.S. Sanitary Commission. Later called "Marshlands," for the Beaufort home depicted by Francis Griswold in his 1931 novel, A Sea Island Lady, it was designated a National Historic Landmark in 1975.

City Hall, on the northeastern corner of Broad and King Streets, is festooned with flags in this *c.* 1917 view. The number of flags indicate a major occasion. (The Charleston Museum Collection, MK 8977B.)

The present gleaming white 1930s Federal Deco-style edifice at 1503 Bay, between Monson and Bladen Streets, which was dedicated as a United States courthouse on November 9, 1994, bears little resemblance to the eclectic Romanesque structure above, upon which the radical remodeling was performed in 1936. This courthouse, whose cornerstone was laid with Masonic rites on November 29, 1883, replaced the original one lost to fire: the four-story, residential "Barnwell Castle," in which Lafayette had been entertained on his visit to Beaufort in 1825.

The cornerstone of the Hampton County Courthouse, built on land donated by Mrs. Josephine A. Hoover, was laid by General Wade Hampton on October 12, 1878, while he was governor of South Carolina. Different in appearance from any other county courthouse in the state, the brick Italianate Victorian structure, which still stands on Main Street, features a second-story arch over its front entrance. In 1925, it underwent major renovations, resulting in the removal of the double curved stairway and the eight interior chimneys.

Approximately 30 plantations had frontage on Lands End Road by the beginning of the War Between the States. Sometimes called the Old White Church, the Chapel of Ease was also situated on the road. It was built about 1740 as an extension of St. Helena's Parish to provide a place for the planters to worship without having to travel to Beaufort.

The Chapel of Ease is considered to be one of the finest remaining tabby structures left in the Lowcountry. After the American Revolution, the chapel was separated from St. Helena's Parish to form a separate church. The building burned in a forest fire in 1886 and was never restored. The ruins were used in a quick shot in the movie *The Big Chill*, which was made during the 1980s.

The Sea Island Hotel, once on the northeast corner of Bay and Newcastle Streets, was erected *c.* 1820 as Scotsman George Mosse Stoney's home, later served as General Saxton's Civil War headquarters, and finally became a commercial hotel for some 80 years. It was razed in 1959 and replaced by the Sea Island Motel in 1960.

The Cope House became the Mayflower Inn when the Brooker family purchased it sometime between 1904 and 1909. Some claimed it as the best hotel in lower Carolina during the early years of the twentieth century. Located on the corner of North Railroad Avenue and Bridge Street as early as 1898, it served several generations of travelers. Later called the Bamberg Hotel, it was demolished in November 1958.

Cassina Point house is pictured here in a scene that is quite unusual for a South Carolina Sea Island. It depicts the "big snow" of 1914—a memorable event! The house is now a bed and breakfast where guests can enjoy a glimpse of Sea Island life as it once was lived.

The Fort Sumter Hotel, built in 1925, rises as the tallest building on the waterfront in this 1936 view of the city. The old bathhouse dock had become the place of swimming and diving for local children who enjoyed the harbor on a summer afternoon. (The Charleston Museum Collection, MK 3335.)

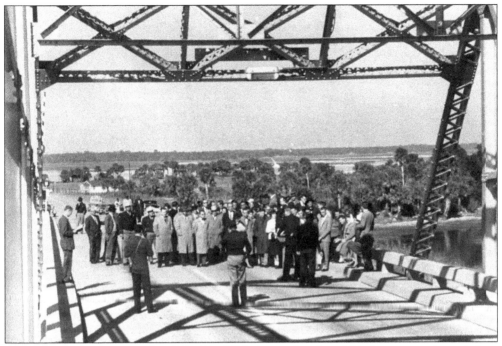

The J. Byrnes Bridge opened on May 20, 1956. A crowd gathered for the ceremonies and then traveled to the Honey Horn property for a celebration. This was the first bridge connecting Hilton Head to the mainland. The cost was $1.5 million. (Coastal Discovery Museum.)

In its first year, 48,000 cars crossed the bridge. At first, the bridge cost $2.50 per round trip. The toll was phased out by 1959. The Byrnes Bridge was a swing bridge. It swung open to allow boats to pass through on either side of the center support. (Ernest Ferguson.)

This view of the single-lane Dawho Bridge shows people waiting for the bridge to be closed before crossing. Since the bridge could not be approached unless the tide had gone down, it created an opportunity to visit with neighbors and could have been the origin of "Edislow" time.

This photo shows the last swing bridge to cross the Dawho River. It has since been replaced by a fine fixed bridge. The old-timers were not too happy with the idea of the new fixed bridge, but it is probable that each "upgrade" in methods of crossing this body of water must have brought the same sort of regrets.

This drawing features the construction of the 1875 lighthouse. Classified as a second order beacon, the structure stands 133 feet above the mean high tide. The only permanent residents on the island were the lighthouse keepers and their families. The lighthouse was taken out of service in 1933 and the compound deeded to Beaufort County. (National Archives.)

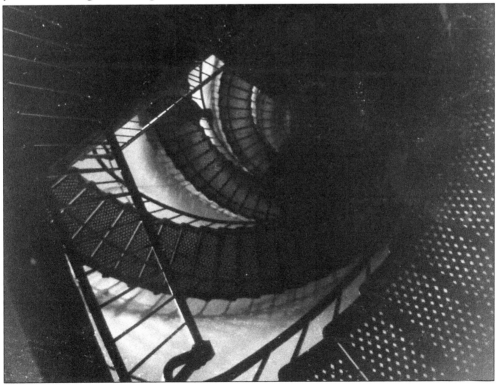

Access to the beacon housing was by walking up a spiral, metal staircase. The bottom step at the entrance of the lighthouse is the first of 185 steps which lead to the beacon room. Visitors today can follow the staircase only to the observation deck just outside the glass housing.

The Hilton Head Lighthouse was originally built by the Coast Guard in the 1870s. This lighthouse was built nearly 1 mile inland, and a smaller range lighthouse was built closer to the beach. Now, it is called the Leamington Lighthouse and is no longer used for navigation. (Parris Island Museum.)

Despite the dense forest and underbrush, the lack of roadways and swamps, mosquitoes and malaria, and fierce animals, the keepers of the light did their job of keeping that light burning. In 1933, the federal government put out the light.

The most recognizable landmark on Hunting Island is the lighthouse. As this drawing from 1874 shows, its major function was to act as a navigational aid for ships. The first lighthouse was built in 1859 and destroyed by Confederate troops during the War Between the States. The second tower was completed in 1875. The lighthouse was moved in 1889 to its present location because of the problems of erosion on the beachfront. (National Archives.)

The small white building to the side of the lighthouse was used for oil storage. The flame for the beacon was provided by burning vaporized oil inside a hollow wick. The paint design on the lighthouse was its signature. Each of the 256 national lighthouses had a unique paint pattern, along with a specific flashing sequence so when a ship's captain saw a light, he would know his location and the dangers he faced.

Five

STREET SCENES

Bay Street.   Beaufort, S. C.

In 1913 the Beaufort Bank bought from Mrs. Scheper the property on which the old Post Office stood and erected the building at the right in this view looking east on Bay Street. The Custom House is probably flying the flag seen here. Years later the bank was used as a movie theater. In 1998, it stood at 926 Bay as the Bank Waterfront Grill and Bar.

This view of Broad Street shows the sometimes-quiet nature of the city. The buildings in the foreground are now sites occupied by First Federal of Charleston. In the distance the portico marks what was the site of the Bank of South Carolina, now the location of the People's Building, constructed in 1910/11. (The Charleston Museum Collection, MK 22692, AWC.)

In a 1933 view of Broad Street, young sidewalk vendors sell Christmas flowers. Note the trees that once lined Broad Street, many of which were lost in the tornadoes of 1938. (The Charleston Museum Collection, MK 9781)

These schoolgirls enjoy an afternoon lunch on the benches in White Point Gardens on May 1, 1939. (The Charleston Museum Collection, MK 17016.)

By standing on the corner of Fishburne and Church Streets, one can see the back of Drawdy's Store on the left and the Bedon-Lucas house on the right. Drawdy's Store was built in 1822 by Ezra Miller. A gas station and convenience store now occupy the space. N.Y. Perry built the house about 1820 and later sold it to Richard Bedon. Mr. Bedon gave the lot in front of the house to the Library Society in 1843 and then sold the house to Clarence Lucas. It remained in the Lucas family until it was purchased by the Colleton County Historical and Preservation Society in 1996. Major renovations are underway, without changing the design, to turn this wonderful old home into offices and meeting spaces for the Society and to create a place for cultural and social events for the community.

This real photo postcard is looking up Washington Street from Lucas Street. Notice the two-way traffic! Next to Belk Hudson, which moved to a larger store at Ivanhoe Shopping Center in August 1973, is Thompson's 5¢ to $1 store. This store still looks like an old-time variety store with items you wouldn't find anywhere else and is closed on Wednesday afternoons. On the right side, Hayes has moved up the street, but is still owned by the Harris family. Mortie Cohen owned Walgreen's Colleton Drugs, and Leon Gelson owned and operated the Western Auto Store. Next to Western Auto is Easterlin's Furniture store owned by W.C. Easterlin.

One can see the water tower in the background. It was completed in 1915 and has a 100,000-gallon capacity. The lower level was originally built as a jail, but it was so damp that prisoners were never detained there. In the late 1940s there were eight druggists on Washington Street: Colleton Drugs (Walgreen Agency), Gibson Kemp Drug Co., Heaton's Drug Store, Ackerman-Beach Drug Store, Kleins Drugs, Padgett's Pharmacy, Peoples Pharmacy, and Walterboro Drug Co. (the Rexall Store). On the left, notice the Western Auto Store, owned by Leon Gelson, next to Easterlin Furniture Co. Beyond Gibson Drugs on the right, one can see Thompson's 5¢ to $1 Store, Belk Hudson, and the Brick Store.

At left in this view of Main Street is the Home Bank building (1910), which in the late 1990s was acquired, renovated, and opened as the Bank of Barnwell County. The unit of stores beyond Blanton's Bakery seen here at right on the north side of the street has disappeared and the space has been turned into a parking lot.

The Gilldare Hotel, seen here at right, is the principal focus of this view of a portion of the south side of Allendale's Main Street. In existence at least as early as 1907, it later became known as the New Warren and stayed in business through the mid-1950s. It can still be seen, with a much modified brick front, on the southeast corner of Main and Railroad. In 1910, the business establishments running east down the block to the bank on the corner included stores for general merchandise, candy, clothing, and shoes.

The courthouse is still visible in the distance in this view of lower Main Street. The sign on the telephone pole at right indicates that the photograph was taken sometime near or during Carnival Week at Christmas time. The sign of the Bamberg Dry Goods Store is clearly legible at the left, and the grocery store next door has set up an informal produce market on barrels and crates in the street out front.

Employees on the upper floors of the Bamberg Cotton Mill watch with other townspeople as the decorated vehicles and their mounted escorts in an unidentified parade, having just crossed Main Street, make their way westward on Elm Street. Denmark photographer E.E. Burson made the picture, which may have been taken around Thanksgiving or Christmas.

The June 28, 1776 victory of patriot forces on Sullivan's Island over a British invasion fleet has been celebrated in South Carolina ever since. Here, at the Old Exchange Building, a crowd of notables, dignitaries, and rather somber Girl Scouts have gathered after the parade down Broad Street. (The Charleston Museum Collection, MK 3216.)

Horse-drawn buggies, automobiles, and bicycles have conveyed the parties to what appears to be a cold, damp gathering, possibly a fall political one. In 1915, Denmark was a town of about 1,250 inhabitants. This rare, limited-issue amateur photograph was made with one or more copies distributed to interested persons.

A large, flag-raising celebration was held inside Fort Sumter on April 14, 1865, four years to the day of the initial Union surrender of Sumter to Confederate forces. The former commander of the fort, Robert Anderson, now a Union general, was on hand to raise the very same flag that he had lowered in 1861. Robert Smalls was also in attendance, arriving at Sumter on his boat, the *Planter*. In this photo, Reverend Henry Ward Beecher, a staunch abolitionist and brother of Harriet Beecher Stowe, addresses the assembled dignitaries. President Abraham Lincoln had planned to attend, but decided not to travel to Charleston, sending in his stead John G. Nicolay, his personal secretary. Later that same day, the President was shot in Ford's Theater in Washington. He died the following day. (E. & H.T. Anthony.)

On the reverse of this postcard, which hosts an advertisement for Stuart & Clancey's drugstore in Beaufort, is a somewhat enigmatic title: "A So. Ca. Turnout—Time 2:26." Perhaps it is a tongue-in-cheek reference to the inherent slowness of the mode of transportation pictured.

During 1902, there were four fire engine companies. Two were white, the Winyahs and the Salamanders, and two were black, the Heston and the Star. The latter Star Fire engine is pictured here. The author dedicates this book to grandfather Albert, Uncles Albert Jr., Herman, Ernest King, Cousin Joseph Crump, and sons Ojas and Obsidian of the King family; many of whom were fire signs.

After the demise of Beaufort's flourishing phosphate industry following the great hurricane of 1893, the county once again depended upon cotton, fish, and timber as economic mainstays. In 1911, Beaufort County ginned 9,904 bales of cotton—the largest number ever remembered being reported for the county—valued at $350,000. Mule-drawn cotton wagons would have been a familiar sight on town and country roads for the first several decades of the twentieth century.

The Union Cotton Compress, at 286 East Bay Street, stood opposite the end of Pickney Street above the city market. Cotton was brought here to be compressed into bales for shipping through Union Terminal to ports around the world. This photograph, made *c.* 1890, is from a booklet entitled *Indelible Photographs* by A. Witteman. (The Charleston Museum Collection, MK 7244.)

An African-American street vendor hurries past number 26 South Battery in this 1930 photograph. Dressed in a suit and boater, he is a purveyor of select okras and tomatoes. (The Charleston Museum Collection, MK 1463.)

A labor crew dug the ditch to install the city of Georgetown's first water sewer system at Front and Wood Streets, the highest ground in town. To function, pipe had to be laid 22 feet deep. The city floated a bond issued for $75,000 for the project, and the system served the city from 1904 until 1992. (Georgetown County Library Morgan Collection.)

Railway Ave., Walterboro, S. C.

There never was a Railway Avenue in Walterboro. The correct name was Railroad Avenue, which ended at the ACL Railway Depot. The house on the left was built by Ben Levy about 1901. The Given's family bought the house in the early twenties. Unfortunately, it burned down in 1988. The "twin houses" built by A.H. Wichman *c.* 1881 were next to this home. Later one of the houses was owned by Dr. Duncan Pagdett. Railroad Avenue was paved in 1921 along with some of the other major streets in Walterboro.

The Atlantic Coast Line Railroad Company connected Walterboro to their main line at Green Pond, 12 miles away. From there one could travel to Charleston or Savannah, Georgia. They had daily freight and passenger service. Early schedules show the train leaving Walterboro at 7:00 a.m. and 1:35 p.m. The conductor was known to look down Railroad Avenue to make sure there were no late stragglers who might miss the train.

Mr. Martin Elbert "Bert" Terry, a section foreman with the Charleston & Western Carolina Railroad, is shown here seated in front of his crew on a mobile service unit along a portion of tracks in the Hampton area. The child sitting on the crossties at right has not been identified. This professional looking, one-of-a-kind view taken at a railroad work site may have been made by an itinerant photographer simply wishing to capture something of the life of railroad men. Or perhaps it was taken by Terry's wife.

A narrow gauge railroad, similar to the one in this photograph, was used to transport the supplies overland from the Johnson's Creek wharf to the lighthouse compound. Old U.S. 21 followed the railbed's path through the maritime forest as it wound its way to the lagoon. The remnants of the dock and walkway are still visible in the marsh. (South Carolina Archives and History.)

A note penned across the verso of this very rare card reads as follows: "Taken in Allendale, S.C. Rae—Charlie and Hap." Here three theatrical troupers, in costume to advertise their evening performance in "Happy Hooligan," pause to have their picture taken next to the train which would have conveyed them on their whistle-stop tour across the region. Allendale, with a 1910 population of 1,200, was probably a frequent stop for traveling shows.

This one-of-a-kind picture of youngsters with their pets and bicycles was typical of the kind of informal portraits which families and individuals had made to mail or to hand out to friends and relations. The two boys with their bikes were the sons of Abe Ruth and Carrie-Lee Ponds Murdaugh, who lived in the western part of the county between Islandton and Ashton. Vernon, at left, died young of appendicitis; Joseph ("J.J."), at right, died in 1970. The boy with the dog was one of the homeless children Mrs. Murdaugh took in and cared for.

Bicycling was all the rage at the turn of the century. Two young women pose with an unusual model for the 1905 photograph. The smaller front wheel was intended to provide easier steering, while the guard on the rear wheel served to prevent the entanglement of skirts and petticoats. (The Charleston Museum Collection, MK 13816.)

Ernest Jerome King (1935–1965) sits on his tricycle just outside of his homestead on Palm Street in Georgetown, 1938.

Animal-drawn vehicles and the bicycle are the principal means of transportation in this view of Bay Street, looking west. To the left are signs indicating the location of Dr. Charles G. Luther's Drugstore and the grocery store belonging to the Kinghorn Brothers.

Henry and Rosa Swinton Hutchinson set out in their shay, or gig. The one-horse shay was a popular means of transportation in the country. It first appeared in Paris in the seventeenth century, and made its way to America as primitive roads were developed.

Homer Phillips, shown here with his horse and buggy, was a member of a large and well-known farm family from the old community of Grays, located in the northernmost reaches of Jasper County and once a part of Hampton County. He later moved to Smoaks. This picture is believed to have been taken by his brother-in-law, photographer Robert Lee Cleland, who lived in Hampton.

This informal outdoor portrait showing two conveyances and their owners at a residential porte cochere is believed to have been taken in Bamberg. It bears the embossed logo of photographer E.E. Burson, who operated a studio in neighboring Denmark from *c.* 1905 to 1920.

Aline Peeples Ayer (1899–1945) and Frank Ayer (1894–1963), who were married in 1924, are shown here (on the far side of the back seat), along with some unidentified friends or relations, in a touring car believed to have been parked at 1 Magnolia Avenue in Hampton. Perhaps the tent here belonged to an itinerant photographer, which this group was visiting. Ayer, from Bamberg, was a veteran's service officer.

Joe Weathers and Bessie Evans, his former girlfriend, take time for a photograph in front of a classic auto. (Thelma H. Weathers.)

Photo op! Sarah and Ritchie Belser sit on the bumper of a 1920s Nash automobile.

Here is a very rare card. In 1922, T.J. McDaniel organized the Coca-Cola Bottling Company in Walterboro. They started out with two mules and a horse, but very soon they were using trucks. Everyone was so proud they took photos. The young driver here just happens to be Julius E. Breland (right). Driving and delivering Coca-Cola was one of his first jobs as a young man. Later with his wife, Reba, they raised two children, Walker and Irene, and ran Breland's Guest House on Jefferies Boulevard. In the 1940s he served on the town council. We have been unable to identify the man standing with Mr. Breland.

The only known surviving picture of Beaufort's early Chinese-American merchant and bottling entrepreneur, Charles Chin Sang (1842–1927), this postcard shows him standing in the doorway of his Bay Street establishment, along with the Chero-Cola delivery truck and its driver, probably a young relative. Sang had come to Beaufort about 1899 from Charleston, where he was a grocer as early as 1877. He eventually returned to Charleston and is buried in St. Laurence Cemetery there.

The funeral procession aboard the ferry is en route to South Island c. 1950.

Mose Hudson and his son, Lynn, stand on the ferry dock at Jenkins Island. Before the bridge was built to connect Hilton Head to the mainland, the island remained isolated. Transportation after arriving on the island was challenging too. Roads were not paved and were often too small for vehicles. Over the years, access to the island has become much easier. (The Propst family.)

The arrival of the automobile led inevitably to the formation of a Highway Commission, charged with developing roadways and thoroughfares for this new mode of transportation. In this 1906 view, the commissioners are about to leave on their inspection tour of the route proposed for the auto speedway to Summerville. In the first vehicle, the chairman, a Major Hemphill, and secretary, a Colonel Cosgrove, are ready to do their duty. Commissioners Storen and Clark in the second car are followed by Commissioner Connell bringing up the rear in his automobile. (The Charleston Museum Collection, MK 996.)

Robertville retail merchant and planter James Clarence Richardson (1852–1931), pictured on horseback with his grandchild Jesse Franklin Causey Jr. (b. 1912), was Jasper County's first state senator. He was elected as a Democrat for the two consecutive terms between 1913 and 1916. Sometime after 1925, he moved to Garnett, some 6 miles to the northwest, and is buried in nearby Black Swamp Methodist Cemetery.

Six

Smiling Faces

Dates were not available for all of the images in this section, but the reader can look at the styles of clothing and get a general idea of the period of each costume. This charming photo of kissin' cousins shows Eliza Reid Bailey and William E. Seabrook.

Big brother Townsend Belser keeps an eye on his young siblings, Sarah and Ritchie, as he relaxes in the hammock. The setting is the porch of a cottage at Sunnyside Plantation with a view of salt marsh and tidal creek.

Charleston in the summertime is, in a word, hot. Life before air conditioning was eased by shade and breeze. Here a mother rocks her baby in the garden in that most valuable possession, the hammock. While fans came into use in the 1920s and air conditioning was introduced as early as the 1920s in movie houses, it was not until the 1960s that air conditioning began to be a feature in homes in the city. (The Charleston Museum Collection, MK 10056.)

These youngsters were identified as Martha Julia Hopkinson, Francis Hopkinson, and Ethel Scarborough Hopkinson at "Red Top" in 1910. They are the children of James and Nona Hopkinson and the grandchildren of James and Carolina Seabrook Hopkinson.

Joan "Shorty" DeLorise, Catherine "Kitty" Weathers, and David and Toni Coley enjoy an outing to the gardens in the late 1950s.

'Twas the night after Christmas in this 1905 photograph, as Frances Sam's friends gathered to enjoy their new toys together. The group of children gathered includes (from left to right) Mary Maybank, Frances Sams, Ruth Simons, Keating Simons, and Don Sams. (The Charleston Museum Collection, MK 7746.)

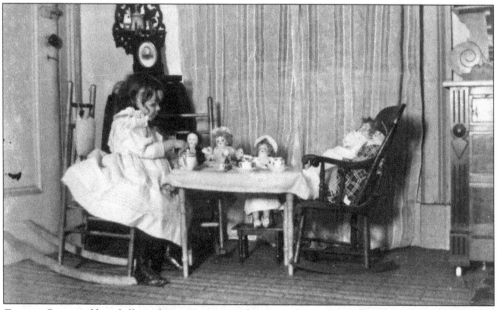

Frances Sams and her dolls sit down to supper at home in this 1902 photograph. (The Charleston Museum Collection, MK 7518.)

These two brothers are surrounded by their animals. A dog is on the left, a cat in the center, and rabbits are in the wagon. It is the winter of 1918.

Two friends at the garden gate have a talk. One, with his bookbag over his shoulder, is off to school. The year is about 1918.

Frances Sams is captured at home by her father. Frances was the model for a number of formal and informal photographs that illustrated the family's domestic activities and pursuits. In this 1895 photograph, she is poised in a doorway at the Sams home on Coming Street. (The Charleston Museum Collection, MK 7518.)

Susan Magette is all dressed up in this photograph c. 1915. (The Charleston Museum Collection, MK 621.)

William Robert Bailey, the son of
Mr. and Mrs. William C. Bailey, is
pictured here in an image from 1914.
He was one of the Edisto Islanders who
served in World War II. He married
an Islander whom he had known
through most of his growing-up years.

This young miss enjoys the porch of her house
as she takes her animals for a ride about 1910.

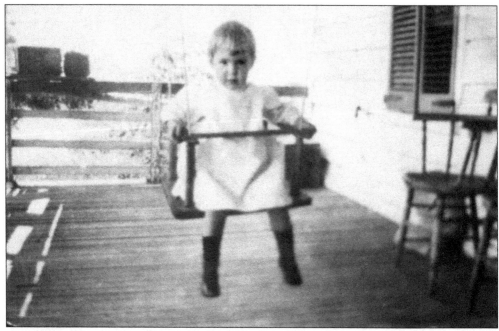

A swing on Grandma's porch was quite safe for the toddler.

Three brothers pose at the photographer's studio in Charleston. Descendants of the original Vennings, these boys stayed in the Village as adults and became good citizens. The photographer, W.B. Austin had the Van Dyke agency.

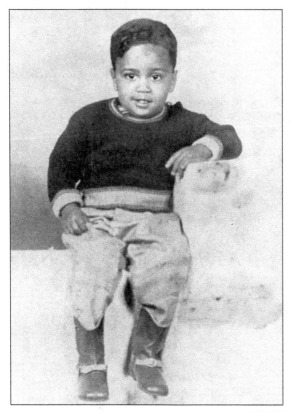

Walter Manigault Sr. used little Walter Jr. for the Walter Manigault Funeral Home Calendar in 1941. He was three years old. This was the first advertisement of its kind in the Georgetown area. Walter Manigault Jr., a 1961 graduate of Eckels College of Mortuary Science, is a licensed embalmer, funeral director, and present owner of the business. (Walter Manigault Jr.)

Dressed in overalls and a straw hat, this little farmer is ready to work. The year is about 1920.

9 781531 665654